3 FOR 30

THREE WORDS OF SCRIPTURE
FOR 30 DAYS

ENLARGE MY HEART

I shall run the way of Your commandments, For You will <u>enlarge</u> <u>my heart</u>. (Psalms 119:32)

My older friend John grew up in a different day. The error of segregation and racism is well documented in American history. He grew up in that history. Unfortunately, the church seemed slow to bring revelation to the body of Christ in this area. It has been said that the most segregated hour in the United States is eleven o'clock on Sunday mornings (I believe that is changing rapidly). John drove an evangelist to the airport after a revival at his church with the aforementioned vantage point. In a moment of transparency, John told the evangelist, "I just don't think I am ready to worship with people so different than myself." The evangelist was gentle but firm. He put his hand on my old friend's shoulder and said, "John, if you can't worship with them here, you may not have a chance up there because every nation, tribe and tongue will be around the throne." The conversation was a turning point for John. He experienced an enlarged heart. He became open to all of God's people. His tenderness and transformation were beautiful things to witness. Shut off hearts are very restrictive. Closed hearts diminish our opportunities to love and grow. People need to go back and untie vows that they have made over the years. These are the bondages that keep hearts small. As we run with the commandments, our hearts are affected. It wasn't just the evangelist that enlarged my friend's heart. He studied the Scripture, and the Word had a tremendous effect. May the Lord enlarge our hearts in all sorts of areas every day moving forward.

On a scale of one to ten (ten being biggest), how big is your heart? Identify an area or two in your life that could use a "heart stretching" or "heart enlargement."

_____

_____

_____

_____

_____

_____

Do you have a Scripture or two in mind that you can run with that enlarges your heart's capacity?

_____

_____

_____

_____

_____

_____

Take a moment to imagine a larger heart. What does it look like? Articulate it.

_____

_____

_____

_____

_____

_____

_____

GO DO TODAY:

Set a timer and spend five uninterrupted minutes asking God to make your heart bigger—a bigger heart like His heart.

WHO MAY ASCEND

Who may ascend into the hill of the LORD? And who may stand in His holy place? (Psalms 24:3)

"Bill really went up the ladder quickly." That statement reflects success. "Second place is the first loser." Ever heard that? Some people are not competitive by nature, but some people will stop at nothing to win. I once was invited to watch my favorite football team play in a big game. The problem with the invitation was that the friend who invited me hated my team and was a fan of the opposing team. I am pretty competitive by nature, myself, but he is even more so. I saw trouble brewing on the horizon. Another couple was invited and I hoped that I wouldn't be a jerk in front of the lovely couple. I certainly didn't see what was coming. The lovely lady (who was actually rooting for my team) kind of went bananas. She got so worked up jawing with the friend who invited me that she couldn't stay for the end of the game. Most people competitively want to go "higher," always striving for that elusive "next level." Some cultural (even Biblical) recipes for ascending into greatness are:

1. Work harder: Get up earlier. Train, train, train. Drink the right sports drink.

2. Think positive thoughts.

3. Have greater confidence: Baseball batters need short memories. That kind of thinking.

4. Dress for success.

5. Leverage your networks.

There you have five of the first ten thousand ways to succeed in modern literature, blogging and philosophy. David places this "next level verse" in the Psalms. _Who may ascend?_ Who gets to the next level? Who wins with God? Who can be His champion? Here you go:

1. Clean-handed and pure-hearted people.

Righteousness ushers us up. Holy thinking. Holy behaving. Not popular ideas. Popularity doesn't matter. These are God-inspired success ingredients.

2. No liars. Lies get people ahead in business and politics. Short term ladder ascension. Rarely do lies hold people in position or keep them climbing. Liars are found out. Certainly lies never let us ascend to that holy place - a place Eugene Peterson translated in his Message Bible as "Mount God." The New Living Translation says people may ascend "who never tell lies."

3. Ascension happens when people refuse to "swear deceitfully," translated as those who will not "worship idols." Jesus said no man can serve two masters. He also said a house divided will not stand. It is hard to—check that—it is impossible to truly worship God AND anything. Never God and

money; God and fame; God and things. According to this chapter, success means people that ascend (that win) will "receive a blessing from The Lord." These competitors will have "a right relationship with God."

So let's review. Who shall ascend? Righteous, truth-telling worshippers of God alone. Peterson says, "God is at their side and with God's help they make it." Winners.

How competitive are you on a scale of 1 to 10—10 meaning most competitive? What number would the people who know you best give you?

_____

_____

_____

_____

_____

_____

Let's keep the same scale. If 10 is the top of the mountain, where do you see yourself today with God?

_____

_____

_____

_____

_____

_____

Look at the big three: righteousness, truth and sincere worship. What needs the most work right now?

_____

_____

_____

_____

_____

GO DO TODAY:

Go higher in your walk with God. No excuses. Write a prayer asking for help.

MAJESTIC IN HOLINESS

Who is like You among the gods, O LORD? Who is like You,
<u>majestic in holiness</u>, Awesome in praises, working wonders?
(Exodus 15:11)

May I be your tour guide for ten minutes? Let's go to Iguazu

Falls. The waterfalls are in the Iguazu River located on the

border of the Argentine province of Misiones and the

Brazilian state of Paraná. For most of its course, the river

flows through Brazil; however, most of the falls are on the

Argentinian side. Part of it forms the boundary between

Argentina and Brazil. Numerous islands along the 1.7-mile

edge divide the falls into many separate waterfalls, 197 to

269 feet high. The number of these smaller waterfalls

fluctuates from 150 to 300, depending on the water level.

There are points in three cities of Brazil, Argentina, and

Paraguay that have access to the Iguazu River. The borders of all three nations may be seen and it is a popular tourist attraction for visitors to those cities. Upon seeing Iguazu, the United States First Lady Eleanor Roosevelt reportedly exclaimed, "Poor Niagara!" At one point a person may stand at Iguazu and be surrounded by 260 degrees of waterfalls. The "Devil's Throat" in Argentina has water pouring into it from three sides. Likewise, because Iguazu is split into many relatively small falls, one may view these, a portion at a time. Often Iguazu also is compared with Victoria Falls in Southern Africa. The physical structure of Victoria does not allow this multiple view experience, as it is essentially one waterfall that falls into a canyon. Iguazu Falls have been portrayed in nearly twenty films including *Moonraker* and *The Mission*. One of the movies dates back to 1907. In 1876, there was only one "national park" in the world: Yellowstone in the U.S.A. When Yellowstone was just four years old, Andre Reboucas, an engineer, proposed that Iguazu become the second such park in the world, stating it had been "created by God," calling it "magnificent" (another descriptor of majestic). On the Brazilian side, there is a walkway along the canyon. Helicopter rides offering aerial views of the falls have been available from Brazil. I have had the great privilege of viewing these Falls not once, but twice, ten years apart. The word for what I saw is, indeed, "majestic." Perhaps you are thinking, "Nice tour, what's the point?" The point is that both times I witnessed this marvel, the experience was "majestic:" characterized by or possessing majesty; of lofty dignity or imposing aspect; stately; grand. Majesty also means regal, lofty, or stately dignity; imposing character; grandeur; supreme greatness or authority; sovereignty. That definition applies to Iguazu Falls. So how does it apply to holiness? Let's tour some of the many definitions of that word. "Holiness" means the quality or state of being "holy." Holy has been defined as: specially recognized as or declared sacred by religious use or authority; consecrated; dedicated or devoted to the service of God, the church, or religion; saintly; godly; pious; devout; having a spiritually pure quality; entitled to worship or veneration as or as if sacred: inspiring fear, awe. I have heard a simple definition of holiness as "completely separated in purity." When I stepped out on the platform at the Devil's Throat and saw the Falls, it took my breath away both times. Complete and utter amazement. We might remember here that God created those Falls. When we step out onto the platform and witness His holiness—the complete and utter purity, separation, supreme greatness, complete and pure quality of inspiring awe of God—it has that same effect. There is a sense of stately dignity, authority and grandeur—*majesty*. On a platform at those God-created falls, every single slight turn of the head brings another gasp. One could drink the views for weeks. God's great holiness is breathtaking and there are new vistas and spectacular sights every time one stands on the viewing platform. He is _majestic in holiness_ and Iguazu is just one of His _working wonders._ YOU happen to be another!

What is the most majestic thing in creation that you have ever seen?

_____

_____

_____

_____

_____

Describe it. Why was it majestic? Use descriptive words.

_____

_____

_____

_____

_____

_____

Would any of those words describe the holiness of God? Use some of them and other descriptive words to describe God's holiness below.

_____

_____

_____

_____

_____

_____

GO DO TODAY:

Go outside and look at something God made for three to ten straight minutes. Something small and intricate like a grasshopper or large and spectacular like a big lake. Either in writing or just in mental exercise, note the amazing aspects. Consider the One who made the thing you just looked at for three to ten minutes and search for the words to express His awe.

SEE THE BLOOD

The blood shall be a sign for you on the houses where you live; and when I <u>see the blood</u> I will pass over you, and no plague will befall you to destroy you when I strike the land of Egypt.
(Exodus 12:13)

In the 1990s, I was a young man serving the Lord in youth ministry. It was just another regular church workday. The office attire was a shirt and tie in those days. During our regular ten minute daily staff devotion, Rev. Max Price, pastor of visitation, was praying for a family whose name I cannot remember. What I do remember is that he prayed and said, "I plead the blood of Jesus over their lives, vehicle, and trip." That decades-ago phrase in a run-of-the-mill meeting from a now-deceased friend deeply affected me. I began to study why Max would pray like that and what the prayer meant. "Pleading the blood" was something that used to be done quite a bit, decades ago. The saints would "plead the blood" over family members, their own homes, businesses, problems, and over virtually anything. The phrase emanates from this Scripture in Exodus. The blood of the lamb was a sign to the death angel that destruction had to "pass over" the house which displayed it. It was a protecting spiritual exercise. I suppose that I have been praying that same prayer nearly every day for my family for decades now. I want the blood of Jesus, the perfect Lamb of God, to mark every member of my family. When the enemy of our soul tries to fulfill his job description (steal, kill, and destroy), I want Satan to see that this house and household is marked by that precious blood of Jesus Christ.

Do you believe in the power of the blood of Jesus Christ?

_____

_____

_____

_____

_____

_____

Who and what is so precious to you that you would want to

pray "the blood over?"

_____

_____

_____

_____

_____

_____

Is praying in this fashion an action that the Holy Spirit may
be directing you towards?

_____

_____

_____

_____

_____

_____

_____

GO DO TODAY:

Begin a month-long process of asking God to cover every
valuable thing in your life with the blood of the Lamb of
God, Jesus Christ. (Warning: It could turn into a life-long
process).

GRACE IS SUFFICIENT

And He has said to me, "My <u>grace is sufficient</u> for you, for power is perfected in weakness." Most gladly, therefore, I will rather boast about my weaknesses, so that the power of Christ may dwell in me. (2 Corinthians 12:9)

"Joe, the thought of what you do for a living makes me feel physically nauseated. I mean I get a visceral reaction when I let myself dwell on what you do for more than a few seconds." That is what a friend of mine said to me about my vocational choice of evangelism. Some friend. Actually he is a fine friend and a good man. He led a denomination's youth ministry for a southern state at the time of our conversation. When my friend thought about the grind of the road, he couldn't take it. Motel after motel. Packing, unpacking, packing, unpacking. The road food. Being absent from the family for days on end. It all made him queasy. My response to him was a little bitter actually. "Buddy, you live on a campground. Your summers are spent at camp. You walk across the driveway to your office. You live, work and do weeks of summer camp in the exact same space. You just leave now and then to buy some supplies down the road. It doesn't make me sick, but it does make me claustrophobic." There is one word that enables each of us—an evangelist and a youth director—to do the things we do. The word is "grace." "Grace" comes from the transliteration of the Greek word, χάρις "Charis." It means favor and kindness. It has often been defined as "God's unmerited favor." It is the dynamic by which we are saved from sins and delivered from the power of it. It seems to me that it is the secret ingredient enabling my friend to live, work, camp and spend all his hours in the same space. That word is the powerful potion that makes this man (me) enjoy the rhythm of truck stops and cheap motels. Grace. Favor and kindness. Paul said it kept him in the game, in spite of weakness. Have you ever looked at a man or woman and thought (or said), "How do they do it?" Perhaps looking at a parent of a special needs child. Maybe looking at a single mom with multiple kids and jobs. I have that thought about leaders, especially Presidents of the United States. "How do they take that much pressure?" Perhaps you are going through something today that might make others shake their head in disbelief. There is a way that you can navigate it all. That way is the way of grace. Lean into the grace that God will provide in your weaknesses. This evangelist loves to be in my home with my family. After a while though, there is an inner impulse that beckons me back to the highway. My friend doesn't share that impulse. You may not either. There is one reason I can do it: Grace. Only one person can do exactly what you have been called to, and it is by the same method. Grace. Grace is sufficient.

In your life, who makes you shake your head in wonder thinking, "How do they do it?"

_____

_____

_____

_____

_____

_____

Name a time in your life that you felt that sufficient grace.

_____

_____

_____

_____

_____

_____

Have you ever tried to do something in your own strength without grace? What was it and how was it?

_____

_____

_____

_____

_____

GO DO TODAY:

Evaluate your biggest challenge. Have you started to lean into the grace God has offered you to rest and work in his will? While our calling is never easy, it can be simplified by resting in his grace. Focus on doing some strong and serious leaning into that grace today.

HE HEALED THEM

And the blind and the lame came to Him in the temple, and <u>*He*</u> <u>*healed them*</u>*. (Matthew 21:14)* [The following story was provided to Jewell Massey, our Prayer Team Leader, and to the other members on the Rescue Prayer Warrior Team at JPM]

My name is Tishia. I'm a young woman from the mountains of Virginia. I would like to take a moment to share a very personal story of mine with you all. A few years into my marriage, my husband and I decided that we wanted to try to have a baby. We said "we won't try, but if it happens, it happens." So I stopped taking my birth control. After about seven months, I still had not gotten pregnant so we really started "trying." I went to the doctor and was told it would be extremely hard for me to get pregnant because of serious physical complications. Although I was distraught, I was persistent in trying, and we started using ovulation kits, checking basal body temps, etc. After another year, I thought I was going crazy. I was dreaming about babies, thinking about babies, talking about babies, crying over babies. My whole life revolved around babies. If I was in church and a mom came in holding a baby, I would cry immediately wondering why God saw fit to give them a baby but not us. If I was in public and saw a bad mom, I would get upset and cry wondering why God would bless an awful mom with a baby instead of blessing a Christian home who would raise children for The Kingdom. I became obsessed and very broken. My husband and I pray together every morning. We have for the six years we have been married. Even during the bad seasons and every day since we decided we were ready, we would pray for a baby. And every month, I would be let down. With every negative pregnancy test, I would slide further and further into a pit that I didn't think I would climb out of. Finally, we decided to go to a specialist. Our appointment was for the first Monday in May. We hadn't told anyone we were going, not even our closest friends. We were very private throughout the whole process. Partly because I'm a very awkward person, partly because I don't like people in my business, but mostly because I didn't want people to know of my "inadequacies." The Sunday before we went, Joe came to our church and an odd series of events that I won't elaborate on happened. To make a long story short, two ladies who didn't even know what was going on both *spoke words of promise* over me that we would have a baby. One of those ladies told me that she felt I needed to get Joe to agree with me in prayer over the situation. With puffy eyes from crying, shaky hands and a shaky voice, I went up to Joe and told him about the situation. He asked for me to get my husband, placed my husband's hands on my abdomen, and we all prayed together. Now I would be lying if I said I felt at peace, but I can say that I felt hopeful. More hopeful than I had throughout the whole journey. That was on May 3rd. On June 10th, I found out that we were very newly pregnant. On February 26th at 11:14 pm, we welcomed Lily Kate Bentley into the world. And while you *Prayer Warriors* all may not think this is that big of a deal because you all see miraculous healing and wondrous things happen all of the time, to us, it's everything, and for that, we want to say thank you and let you know that your prayers matter, your prayers make a difference, and your prayers create miracles.

And to conclude my small novel, this past week Joe came back to Zion and I waited until the last night of the conference and walked up to Joe and said, "I know you probably don't remember us..." And he smiled and cut me off and said, "actually I do. Is this the baby?" I started crying.

He healed them.

Do you think it is okay to feel angry at God during physical crises? Why? Why not?

_____

_____

_____

_____

_____

_____

Have you ever felt that sting of "why me" that Tishia described? When? Why?

_____

_____

_____

_____

_____

What is the greatest physical miracle or healing that you can remember seeing or hearing about in your close circle of friends or family?

_____

_____

_____

_____

_____

_____

_____

GO DO TODAY:

Ask God in a focused prayer to heal someone you know. Ask God to heal you in your own body if you need to be healed.

NO WORTHLESS THING

I will set <u>no worthless thing</u> before my eyes; I hate the work of those who fall away; It shall not fasten its grip on me. (Psalms 101:3)

My "Grammy" lived in a lovely model home near a lake in southern Alabama. There was no cable for television so she saved Social Security money to buy a satellite dish that seemed as large as something the Pentagon might have. Grams watched Christian Television and professional wrestling. As a teenager, I found odd similarities between the two. Whenever she went to bed, there were adults in the house visiting that could move the satellite around and find some of the vilest programming imaginable. Same equipment. Vastly different outcomes. Gospel shows had merit. "Adult programs" were "worthless."

worthless (*adj.*) 1. without practical value or usefulness

2. without merit; good-for-nothing.

Walk through a mall food court. Conduct a quick survey. What percentage of people will be looking at their devices? Thirty percent? Fifty? If the mall is not occupied by senior adults, it might be 85% or higher. If we had omniscience like God, it would be fascinating to ascertain the percentage of objects viewed in said devices as "good-for-nothing." How many squirrel pictures, restroom selfies, Starbucks cups, game invitations, bizarre dancing, wedding fail videos, dogs barking at mirrors, feet in sand, kids flipping out at doctors and the like do we need to see to advance as a civilization? Some synonyms of *worthless* are: bogus, futile, inconsequential, ineffective, insignificant, meaningless, mediocre, pointless, unimportant, unproductive, unprofitable, useless, cheap, empty, and counterproductive. What is before your eyes? The antonyms for *worthless* are: beneficial, fruitful, helpful, important, meaningful, productive, profitable, significant, useful, valuable, worthwhile, worthy. That is a pretty good litmus test for what to view on your television, computer, phone, tablet, or whatever technology provides us next. Does the image add value to your destiny? Here are some takeaways:

What is in front of your eyes regularly that adds value to you?

_____

_____

_____

_____

_____

_____

_____

_____

What is regularly before your eyes that is futile, pointless and unproductive?

_____

_____

_____

_____

_____

What action might the Holy Spirit be directing you towards for greater life profit?

_____

_____

_____

_____

_____

GO DO TODAY:

Take an inventory. Determine what has no value. Eliminate it.

KNOW MY PATH

*When my spirit was overwhelmed within me, Thou didst <u>know</u>
<u>my path</u>. In the way where I walk They have hidden a trap for
me. (Psalms 142:3)*

The missionary thought it would be a fun idea to go on a
midnight jungle hike with 225 Singaporean students in
Malaysia. "Why not?" I thought. "It might be fun." It proved
not to be; however, it did prove to be memorable. I was the
speaker for the National Youth Convention in Singapore. We
took nice busses several hours north of Singapore into
Malaysia. The convention was a great experience made
greater by having my twelve-year-old son, Joseph, with me.
The hike started out as exciting. However, we found
ourselves stuck on the trail. No one was moving. No one and
not an inch. In the year 2000 there were no cell phones on

the trail except for the Superintendent of the denomination. He was chatting with his daughter at a Minnesota university as memory serves. To set the scene, imagine eyeballs from the jungle staring at you. If that were not freaky enough, introduce into the scene random loud monkey sounds. Introduce discussion of wild tigers. Dark. Creepy. Standstill. No communication. What we would find out much later was that there was a mud slide at the front of a very long single file line. Few humans are as "citified" as people from Singapore. There are 5.4 million people in the city—which doubles as a country—about 3.5 times as large as Washington D.C. My son and I were at the very back of the line. We had to wait on 220 urbanites to scale up an eight-foot embankment. Excitement turned to adrenaline. Soon adrenaline graduated to confusion, exhaustion, fear, and frustration. My now adult son recalls, "I just wanted to live." Beyond the lack of communication, we were faced with these two significant facts: 1) We had no idea what was going on. 2) We could not go back. Maybe that is exactly where you are right now. You have no idea what is happening on your path. It is painfully apparent that you are too far down the path to turn back now. Insert the promise. God knows the path. He knows the jungle. The traps. What is behind the eyeballs shining in the leaves. Where the noises are coming from. God knows the delays and further what is causing the delays. If someone hovered over us that night in a helicopter at 2 a.m. with soldiers in infrared head gear, they would have immediately known what the problem was. I can almost hear in my head what the chatter would have sounded like over the radios. "There are a couple hundred Asian teenagers and a huge American at the end. Not moving. Follow the line. Oh, see there, they have to help the teenagers over the muddy ravine one by one. This might take all night." God hovers over the hoverers. He sees it all. There may be a reason you are not moving right now. Stay the course. God knows the path because he made it so trust in his vision. He can see at midnight even when you cannot. Commit your path to the Lord in the midst of feeling overwhelmed and not knowing what could trip you up ahead. He will not let you fall.

When was the last time you felt like you didn't have a handle on what was happening on your path?

_____

_____

_____

_____

_____

_____

_____

_____

How did that lack of control make you feel?

_____

_____

_____

_____

_____

_____

Take comfort in God's infrared OMNISCIENCE and whisper

a thank you (a written whisper) that He knows your path

today.

_____

_____

_____

_____

_____

_____

GO DO TODAY:

Look at an atlas or map (or pull up one online if there are none around) and stare at it. Imagine that God knows every single village, city, berg, hamlet, tree, and road sign. Extend that thought to your own path right this minute.

AROSE ANOTHER GENERATION

All that generation also were gathered to their fathers; and there <u>arose another generation</u> after them who did not know the LORD, nor yet the work which He had done for Israel.
(Judges 2:10)

I drive lots and lots of miles every year. Generally, it doesn't bother me. On any given early Sunday morning, I actually enjoy an open road at dawn without much traffic. It clears the head and calibrates the day for me. However, there are a few times when driving isn't much fun. It is not fun to drive in inclement weather. It isn't fun when there is an unforeseen construction issue or traffic backup. Driving is never fun when the traffic is so thick that maneuvering is impossible and there is an eighteen-wheeler a quarter of an inch from the back of my truck and closing in. I hate being pushed by weather, traffic, the clock, and by truckers trying to make their cargo drop on time. Do you like being pushed? I don't. I don't like looking behind me on a disc golf course to discover someone is impatiently pushing me to go faster. Don't look behind you if you hate being pushed. I have some bad news. Something is barreling down on you. It is bigger than a semi-truck. The entity pushing you is known as the next generation and it is closing in fast. Tom Brokaw wrote a book about the greatest generation. There have been some great ones and some not so great ones. But the guaranteed fact is that there will always be a *next* generation until the Lord wraps up this earth for a new earth. They push us. Perhaps we respond like a driver on the interstate with irritation or a golf foursome being pushed by younger golfers. This devotional entry is a proposal to respond to this pushing generation differently. Look at that terrifying verse above. The next generation *did not know* the Lord. Who is responsible for that? Could it be the previous generation? Someone dropped the ball. The generation that did not know the Lord was captured because of their horrific sin. They "prostituted themselves" to other gods and consequently, they were in "great distress" and in "disaster." The worship of filthy "Baals" and disgusting "Ashtoreth" poles put the pushing generation into bondage. Let's rewind the game film and see where the blocks were missed. Who missed their assignment and whose job did not get done? Perhaps we can learn from mistakes so that the generation pushing the reader will not wind up in bondage. Could we change the game by implementing some of these adjustments? 1. Let's tell the generation behind us about our stories. Who the Lord is to us. How we met Him and what our relationship of love is like. 2. Let us live authentically on the tee boxes and roadways in front of them. Students have always been savvy. For decades, I have suggested that many people can be fooled, but one of the hardest to fool is a young person— especially today. If we are hypocritical or disingenuous, that will cause the pushing generation to want nothing to do with the Lord. 3. Let's pray for them often. We don't want to go to heaven and leave behind a hell for the next generation to navigate. Distress, disaster, and bondage. "Lead us not into temptation" is still a daily and relevant prayer. Let's include the next generation as part of "us." One of my mentors, Dr. Mark Rutland, recounts his mother's advice when moving to so many towns during his childhood. As the father's military career took them to yet another town she would say, "Mark, always leave the flower beds better than you found them." May God help us set up the *next generation* to *know the Lord* deeper and more profoundly than even our own wonderful experiences.

Look behind you. Who is pushing you from the next generation? What are their names—those younger than you who may be looking at your life for influence?

_____

_____

_____

_____

Can you add to Joe's list? Besides telling, living, and praying, is there something else practical that may be done so that the "up and comers" truly know the Lord?

_____

_____

_____

_____

_____

Do you see evidence behind you that the next generation is getting closer to God or is it drifting further away?

_____

_____

_____

_____

_____

_____

GO DO TODAY:

Make a conscious decision to at least do these three today: 1) Tell someone in the next generation that there is actually a wonderful God whose name is the Lord. Even a couple of sentences about what He means to you. 2) Be authentic. Live and tell that even when you "miss the mark," you still know that God is real and He doesn't treat us as our sins deserve. 3) Say a prayer.

PLACE TO WEEP

Joseph hurried out for he was deeply stirred over his brother, and he sought a <u>place to weep</u>; and he entered his chamber and wept there. (Genesis 43:30)

Are you an ugly crier? I am. I meet some folks who cry pretty. They are dainty and dab tears in a genteel fashion. When I weep, it is ugly. It's a shoulder shaking and nasty crying situation. It is a "looking for a place to hide" kind of happening. Most of us are prepared for the big potential weeping moments. Moments like funerals and weddings. There are, however, moments that catch us off guard. I visited my in-law's in-law once in the Deep South. I just did it on a whim. I knew the dear saint was older, in a nursing home and pretty ill. There was nothing particularly inspiring about that nursing home visit. There were no revelations or miracles. However, something about that visit must have been meaningful to the Lord because His glory filled the cab of my truck as I drove away. It was so amazing that I had to pull over and find a place to weep. Those weeping places are precious. The weeping place was important enough in the life of Joseph for the event to make it into Holy Scriptures. Those weeping places are cathartic. Someone said that tears cleanse the soul. There may be something to that. I remember my own places of weeping from Bogota, Colombia to Hickory, NC. From Montgomery, AL to the hills of Appalachia. A weeping place in the woods started a chain of events a few years ago that changed my life forever. A weeping place at an altar was once a prelude to a literal and actual heavenly vision. Don't waste those weeping places. Joseph was so moved that he sought out a place to weep. If a moment catches you off guard and you feel a good cry coming, seek out your place. Real men and real women know how to seek out a weeping place.

What hits your mind first when you remember your

weeping place?

_____

_____

_____

_____

_____

_____

Consider for a moment your heritage and history. What has

framed your concept of weeping? Have you any male or

female examples of godly, sincere weeping?

_____

_____

_____

_____

_____

_____

Do you think you weep too much or too little? Is there anything you can do to adjust that paradigm appropriately?

_____

_____

_____

_____

_____

_____

_____

_____

GO DO TODAY:

Go find a place to cry really good for about five or ten minutes. If you don't cry, at least you gave an opportunity to find a place to weep.

SHALL BE DONE

"Again I say to you, that if two of you agree on earth about anything that they may ask, it <u>shall be done</u> for them by My Father who is in heaven." (Matthew 18:19)

Modern technology is a marvel! My grandparents would not have imagined in their wildest dreams saying these words into a telephone or gadget, "Route me to 148 Hickory Street." To be directed to a location without ever looking at a map or taking their eyes off of the road would have seemed like science fiction. Amazing indeed. In my line of work—constant traveling—it is a very helpful tool. The Global Positioning System (GPS) voice affirms the completion of my requests in various ways. My recent favorite response is when the mystery lady voice says, "Done!" after I give an instruction. It is spoken with definite authority. In fact, I flinched a little in surprise the first time I heard it. My immediate thought was, "That's what I'm talking about. Get it done, mystery lady. I like it." Jesus gave us a definitive promise in today's Scripture. The promise regards the awesome power of agreement. If two humans can agree on something, the Celestial Positioning System (Heaven's great assurance) is "Done!" To activate this "done" promise, some things have to first be achieved. First, one human being has to recognize a need. Then, the human has to believe that there is value in praying to an invisible God. Next, another person has to be inserted into the scene. That individual may not have the same need, but they must share a simple, albeit powerful faith in the same God. Finally, these two individuals must <u>agree</u> that God will accomplish the request as they pray. So it might work like this. A woman has a great burden about a personal family issue. A spark of faith lights in her heart that God may be able to change the situation or at least change the lack of peace in her heart. God brings to her mind an older friend with lots of faith. She calls. A coffee conference is scheduled for the next morning. This burdened woman shares her heart with a trusted older friend. That similar spark of faith lights within the older woman's heart. She also believes that God is concerned about the personal family issue harassing the younger friend. After a few affirming statements and expressions of confidence, they make their way to the parking lot. Near the dear older saint's car, heads are bowed, hands are clasped, and agreement is made. Done. The voice, louder than a mystery woman's voice from a smart phone, speaks to hearts: shall be done. A driver may not be sure what roads the GPS is taking them on in their journey to a destination, yet they are comforted that it is done. Similarly, the young woman may not know how the issue will be resolved. She may not know the outcome of this personal family need. She may not comprehend the pathway of personal peace awaiting the resolution. But she hears the promise, closes her eyes and thinks, "That's what I'm talking about."

What is your greatest personal burden right now?

_____

_____

_____

_____

_____

Who is the trusted friend you could call for a conference?

Do they have the spark of faith and the willingness to agree

with you? Write down their name.

_____

_____

_____

_____

_____

Now think of someone whom you could agree with as a trusted friend for their need. You may not share their burden, but you could lend your faith. Write down their need.

_____

_____

_____

_____

_____

_____

_____

GO DO TODAY:

Agree in prayer with someone about your need and theirs.

Do it. Call. Visit. Agree.

SEEING THEIR FAITH

"And they brought to Him a paralytic lying on a bed. <u>Seeing their</u> <u>faith</u>, Jesus said to the paralytic, "Take courage, son; your sins are forgiven." (Matthew 9:2)

"Well, I learned something very interesting about you today from your son," said the second grade teacher of my son Joseph. Nothing really strikes fear in one's heart like an adult with a smirk on their face discussing a previous conversation with one's offspring. "Oh no. What was today's revelation?" With some small bit of flare, she continued, "Your son informed the entire class that you could easily be a millionaire because you're so talented, but you chose to be a minister instead." We enjoyed a good chuckle and a head shake. Well, that was only slightly embarrassing. There were more embarrassing revelations from his childhood, I'm quite sure. Like for example, the time when he was three and warned an older pastor with a reputation for fumbling books and coffee (my previous boss!) on stage not to "drop my baby sister." That one was in front of one thousand people at an infant dedication service. Of course, one thousand people incorrectly became instant experts in their perceptions of our family dinner conversations. I truly don't know where my son got the impression that I had million-dollar talent, but to be honest, it made me smile. I liked that my boy thought his dad had such ability. We know from the entirety of Scripture that *faith* is pleasing to our Father. I believe God the Father smiles when His children believe that He can do anything for anybody—that He can fix all our bikes and heal all our boo boo's. One of my favorite verses on faith is this one: *And without faith it is impossible to please God, because anyone who comes to him must believe that he exists and that he rewards those who earnestly seek him* (Hebrews 11:6 NIV). Here are a couple of quick definitions of faith: 1. confidence or trust in a person or thing. 2. belief that is not based on proof. It is a very big deal, this thing we call *faith*. It is the thing that gives us entry into heaven (see Ephesians 2:8). It is a shield that overcomes the trickery and diabolical strategies of Satan (see Ephesians 6:16). When Jesus was asked what was the best "work of God," He answered with the word "believe" (see John 6:29). Faith moves mountains—great obstacles—in our lives (see Mark 11:23). We could spend the rest of the day talking about how important this "belief not based on proof" is (see Hebrews 11:1 in various translations). When it comes to faith, apparently Jesus can *SEE* it! Since He is God, I suppose He sees everything. Two verses later it says, *"Jesus, knowing their thoughts..."* How did he "see" faith? Because of their thoughts? Certainly. Of course the BED helped! Friends wanted a friend healed. When they brought that friend to Jesus on a bed, faith was observed. Once, I watched about a dozen of my students praying for a person without a leg in Brazil and asking God to give the man one supernaturally. I didn't see another leg that day but I certainly SAW faith that day. They really believed God could and would do it! Does Jesus see your faith? When you and I want something or need something and still put needed money as a tithe, offering, or a benevolence gift into an offering bucket, we are saying, "Dad has all the talent in the universe." Jesus sees that. He saw a widow put everything in an offering once, and he wanted his followers to *see* what he was seeing. When the news is so bad that you nearly feel too paralyzed to get out of bed, but you do, because you have "confidence in a person," Jesus sees it. When Hell unleashes a barrage against you, but you tenaciously hold onto promises like a person holding onto a light pole in a hurricane, well, Jesus *seeing faith* responds in love and power. Let Jesus *see your faith* today and walk in the miracle of it.

With the above three-word devotional in mind, think of someone who demonstrated faith that you could see. Who was it? Describe what you saw as faith.

_____

_____

_____

_____

_____

Has anyone ever *seen your faith,* do you think? Who, why, and what circumstances?

_____

_____

_____

_____

_____

How can Jesus specifically see your faith today?

_____

_____

_____

_____

_____

_____

_____

GO DO TODAY:

Read Mark 11:23. Read it one more time. Now, read it a third time. Go somewhere private and out loud, from your own mouth, speak to the mountains and order them to be removed. Order them a second time. Order them a final time.

TRUST IN CONFUSION

No one sues righteously and no one pleads honestly. They <u>trust in confusion</u> and speak lies; They conceive mischief and bring forth iniquity. (Isaiah 59:4)

There is a movie called "Changing Lanes." Doyle Gibson is played by Samuel L. Jackson. William Hurt plays Doyle's sponsor. One of my favorite moments in the film is on a sidewalk outside of a bar. Doyle Gibson has lost his temper and his mind over a series of unfortunate setbacks. On the sidewalk, he angrily says, "I didn't have a drink!" The sponsor reacts dramatically with a few lines. Then he says something that has always stuck with me. "You know booze isn't really your drug of choice anyway. You're addicted to chaos. For some of us, it's coke. For some of us, it's bourbon. But you, you got hooked on disaster." Then he cursed, which of course, I do not recommend. I do not recommend getting hooked on disaster, either. I know people like that and I have fought my entire life against that addiction. Do you know people that have chaos as their default setting? Some people become experts at mystifying dysfunction if they have been around it for years. The sunny days are true anomalies. They know right around the corner, trusted confusion will make its appearance. Trust. It means "reliance on the integrity, strength, ability, surety of a person or thing; confidence." Confusion. It means "disorder; upheaval; tumult; chaos." Imagine people who rely on the strength and ability of disorder, upheaval and chaos. I know these people and do not feel in any way superior. My heart hurts for them because for many years now I have relied on the integrity, strength and ability of God, the Lord whom I serve and love. But for the grace of God, as the saying goes, I would need a twelve step sponsor helping me off of the disaster train. Today you will choose to trust in a person or thing. Don't let it be confusion. There is a better way. There is a better One.

(Creatively change the names) Put the (changed) names of a person, or four people, that you know who seem to be addicted to chaos.

_____

_____

_____

_____

_____

What are some characteristic words that would describe their lives, attitudes, actions or reactions?

_____

_____

_____

_____

Devoid of arrogance or superiority, write a pledge below that you will be addicted to and trust only in God, His power, and His great love for you.

_____

_____

_____

_____

_____

_____

_____

_____

GO DO TODAY:

Take an inventory and if there is an ounce of drama addiction, renounce it and aggressively determine to walk in peace.

DO SOMETHING NEW

Behold, I will <u>do something new</u>, Now it will spring forth; Will you not be aware of it? I will even make a roadway in the wilderness, Rivers in the desert. (Isaiah 43:19)

Driving around with my father-in-law, Jimmy Griggs, before he died was like driving with a professor whose expertise was the city of Columbus, Georgia. The facts would fly quicker than the brain could process. "That used to be nothing but woods." All I could see was businesses stretched in every direction. "This was considered way out in the country when I was a boy." The area he pointed to was now a seasoned residential hub and considered an in-town fixture. He would talk about schools and trees. People long dead he spoke of with detail as if he had just gotten off a party-line phone with them. I was always interested but processed the data with a twinge of sadness. "That was then. Now must be better," I would silently muse. These days, I catch myself giving the same kinds of lectures to my half-interested kids about different parts of the southeast. "Why, in my day this was nothing. Now, it's a top three tourist attraction in the state." Stuff like that. I feel a little sadness while I am saying it. I've discovered that God is always up to something new. He is called the "Ancient of Days," but I cannot imagine Him calling the angels together and saying, "In my day, there used to be nothing until I spoke it. Those were the good ol' days." God has asked us to "be still and know that He is God." He has asked us to do the work of the Kingdom which is to actively believe. God is not idle. He is at work and active. He does new things. He has told us that faith without works is dead. So we become aware that as good as things might be, hold on, there is something new coming. The Christian has the great hope that Heaven is coming and it will be awesome. If things are really bad, hold on, God is at work. He is going to do something new. No matter how amazing a church may be, there is always a new and fresh wind about to blow to touch a previously unrealized person or unrecognized need. A long time ago, I was listening to a teaching from the great professor Howard Hendricks from Dallas Theological Seminary on a tape (yes, a tape; I mentioned it was a long time ago). He told a story that I will paraphrase, openly confessing that my details may be sketchy. This is how I remember it. One of his childhood Sunday school teachers was found dead in her nineties beside her kitchen table. The first responders found a notebook on the table near her body. At the top of the ninety-year-old woman's notebook in bold letters was the heading: "My Goals for the Next Ten Years." The take away is this: no matter how old one gets, there is an awareness that God is doing new stuff and we don't cling to status quo and tradition. Look out, God is going to *do something new.*

Do you know anyone that is fixated on the good old days, not recognizing that God is up to something new? Even young people do that. "The only boy I'll ever love..." stuff.

_____

_____

_____

_____

_____

Have you ever caught yourself wanting to stay in one period of your history forever? When and where?

_____

_____

_____

_____

_____

Read this verse: *That is what the Scriptures mean when they say, "No eye has seen, no ear has heard, and no mind has imagined what God has prepared for those who love him."* (1 Corinthians 2:9 NLT) How might that apply to the "something new" for you?

_____

_____

_____

_____

_____

GO DO TODAY:

Do some good or valuable thing for someone that you have probably never or have almost never done something for before (like cook for your family, rake a widow's yard, buy an acquaintance a gift, etc.). Imagine that just as they didn't see it coming, God has something for you that you don't see coming.

NUMBER OUR DAYS

So teach us to <u>number our days</u>, That we may present to You a heart of wisdom. (Psalms 90:12)

People who are close to me or our ministry know that Jimmy Griggs, my deceased father-in-law, was a very precious person to me. I've mentioned him before in this devotional. He was the patriarch of faith for the family. His salvation and transformation were dramatic. I dedicated my first book to him. Jimmy was born two years before the Great Depression that came upon the United States and affected the world. I have always believed that hearing the stories from his mother and uncles shaped and formed his world view. It affected his actions in various ways, including small ways. At dinners, if there was food left, he often got permission to bring some home. He was as generous of a man as I have ever met. Genuinely. He wasn't a miserly hoarder. He just remembered as a small boy when food wasn't readily available. The cabinets were always full of recycled coffee cups from fast food restaurants and napkins too. That extra ketchup packet (or twelve) was in the refrigerator. Perhaps subconsciously there lived a real threat that maybe ketchup would be scarce in the future. I refuse to judge the behavior or perceptions, because the little recessions I've survived pale against the darkness of those Depression days. In this day, people waste food by the literal ton. Recently I heard of a school district that throws obscene amounts of food away every day. That would have been anathema (detested and loathed) during the Depression. People have the freedom to waste resources when they seem readily available. That mindset creeps into the behavior of practically every generation. Young people especially feel that they are going to live forever on this earth. Why would they ever *number their days* when they look into the "day cupboard" and see it stocked with an endless supply? Wisdom from God is that our days are indeed numbered. As of this writing, I have lived 18,694 days. The average life expectancy in America for males is around seventy-six years. That means I have 9,046 days left if I'm average. (Excuse me a minute while I google anti-depression homeopathic remedies. I'm joking.) In truthfulness, no one is promised another day. There is an appointment for all of us according to Hebrews 9:27. We die and then we are judged. Children die. Babies die. Some people live very, very long lives. The Bible talks about people living hundreds of years. In recent history, a woman named Jeanne Calment died in France on August 4, 1997, at 122 years, 164 days. That is 44,694 days! Yikes. That is a big number. The authorship of much of the Psalms is attributed to David. However, the verse above is a prayer of Moses. Regardless, the Scripture is inspired by the Spirit and the exercise is not meant as a morbid activity to depress us. Nor is it meant as a motivation to hide the napkins in the cupboard. Rather, it is to assign value to the precious life God has given us. There is not an endless supply. I recently went to a wedding and it was promoted in various ways. One interesting way was with a countdown timer. "Only 3 weeks, 2 days, 4 hours, 8 minutes and 16 seconds until we become man and wife!" I look at life a bit like that. If we will ask the Lord to TEACH us to *number our days,* that activity might take us to another level. It assigns value. If Moses is indeed the one who prayed this, let's remember that God used him mightily when he was an older man. Even if we have only a few days left, let's make the most of them!

Consider the number of days that you have lived. If you had to make a guess, what percentage of those days have you "wasted?"

_____

_____

_____

_____

_____

What practical changes could happen in your own experience if you regularly _"numbered your days?"_

_____

_____

_____

_____

_____

Do you think <u>numbering your days</u> would bore you? Why or why not?

_____

_____

_____

_____

_____

GO DO TODAY:

Do some math. Fill out the following formula to determine the number of your days:

1. Multiply your current age by 365.
2. Determine how many days it has been since your last birthday (look at a calendar if you need to.)
3. Add the results from #1 and #2. This gives you your current age in days.
4. Google "life expectancy." Find out what it is for your

gender and country. Add or subtract for your health

circumstances, situation, and hopes.

5. Multiply your "life expectancy" from #4 by 365. This

gives you your life expectancy in days.

6. Subtract your result from #3 (age in days) from your

result from #5 (life expectancy in days).

7. Congratulations, you have numbered your days!

This is the number of days you might realistically

have left. However, of course, only God really

knows.

COMFORTS THE DEPRESSED

But God, who <u>comforts the depressed</u>, comforted us by the coming of Titus...(2 Corinthians 7:6)

Gut punches. September 11, 2001 was a national gut punch. It is a national day of remembrance. A day of depression for some. Personally those were some of the worst seventeen days of my adult life. Three major gut punches in just over two weeks. One of my wonderful mentors suddenly dropped dead far too young in a restaurant. That August 26, 2001, tragedy left me and my wife reeling. Then, on September 10, I discovered that one of my greatest life mentors was living a double life. I had to confront the brutal truth with a hard and bold response. I was devastated. The next day, Tuesday, planes crashed into buildings and horrific devastation happened. I am not a depressive person by nature. All of us have bad days now and again. Trying my best to stay strong, I found myself settling into emotional quicksand. The more I struggled to free myself, the more exhausted and buried I became. At breakfast on Saturday, September 15, I was reading an Atlanta, GA newspaper and noticed one of my favorite preachers, Dr. Mark Rutland, was going to be at a metro Atlanta church the next day. I was scheduled to speak in South Carolina for a Monday engagement. I thought I might like to attend Dr. Mark's service. I was so depressed on that Saturday that I literally could not smile for a previously scheduled family photo shoot in the yard. I tried to, but I looked ridiculously fake. Ever been there? That evening, driving around the Atlanta airport, the security was like a military zone; therefore, I got to the service late. I was so late that I thought I had probably missed it. However, Dr. Rutland had just gone to the pulpit when I arrived. When he was finished, people were lingering around the altar. Mark

Rutland came to me and said, "I've been wrong before and I will be wrong again, but I believe The Lord just told me to tell you this: 'I'm about to give you your joy back.'" Then he prayed for me. Something happened to me and it happened deep inside of me. The Lord God comforted this depressed boy deeply that day. Mark Rutland was my "Titus" that day. In fact, from that day until this, I have never been in that deep quicksand again. Bad days? Sure. Quicksand? Never again. He _comforts the depressed_.

What kinds makes you feel discouraged?

_____

_____

_____

_____

_____

_____

Imagine someone now that *you* could have a "Titus effect"

upon. Write the possibilities.

_____

_____

_____

_____

_____

Claim that comfort promise from God like a sinking man

grabs a rope. Write a bold declaration of that promise

below. "I declare and proclaim that...

_____

_____

_____

_____

_____

_____ "

GO DO TODAY:

Target someone today that in the next seven days, you will be God's instrument to encourage them through a personal touch of some kind (note, visit, post, lunch, etc.).

BE HOLY YOURSELVES

...but like the Holy One who called you, <u>be holy yourselves</u> also in all your behavior (1 Peter 1:15)

When I was doing youth ministry, our best marketing program was "word of mouth." Some of our best marketers were parents. Our policy was that every parent had an invitation to attend one service per year. I didn't want a room full of parents as we ministered to students. About four per week witnessing the service and telling their hairdressers and neighbors was good with me. One Wednesday, a parent came to ask if they could make their visit that particular night. I said "sure," but reminded the dad of the loose rules of the program. "You are a spectator and not a participant in the events that take place tonight." There were about eighty students there that night as I recall. During a sharing time, I noticed the visiting father's hand up. I tried to ignore it. It stayed up. I reluctantly called on the dad. He said, "I wasn't going to say anything (to which I should have said, 'Good. Don't!'), but I have been about to explode. I know this is a youth service but this is still God's house. People are coming in here with ball uniforms on and ball caps. You should be ashamed." Well, I certainly was ashamed for his son who was in the room. The parent was a good man and the son was a great kid. So as not to embarrass the student, I simply acknowledged his "request" with a head nod and a "does anyone else have a prayer request?" In essence he was right. That was God's house. We should revere the sanctuary. While he was speaking, I saw my leaders pulling off caps from their construction jobs (and looking at their hair, one was inclined to yell "put the hats back on!"). I had been working on some local athletes for months, and they were convinced that coming straight from baseball practice was a worthwhile endeavor. They wore hats also. Following the service and away from people, I confronted this father. I told him that he had violated the rule and authority of leadership—a patently unbiblical activity. I told him that I noticed his wife had on slacks. The Independent Church a couple of miles away would not let her in God's house that way. The Pentecostal Holiness Church would have had a hard time letting her worship with her make-up on. I mentioned other faiths that would take umbrage with her hair style and her jewelry. So I asked, "Who made you the hat rule guy?" In fact, some places would throw a flag of violation because his wife was NOT wearing a hat. The call for us to be holy is complicated. It is too complicated to cover in a devotion, or series of books for that matter. Leonard Ravenhill said, "When there is something in the Bible that people don't like, they call it 'legalism.'" Of course there should be boundaries. The Bible even in the New Testament had boundaries (see Acts 21:25). The word "holy" means 1. specially recognized as or declared sacred by religious use or authority; consecrated. 2. dedicated or devoted to the service of God, the church, or religion. That is broader than wearing ball caps. Yet the definition includes what is worn, eaten, watched, worshipped and so much more. If we want to be dedicated and devoted to God, taking our hats off in church shouldn't be a big deal. I saw someone this week preach to a sanctuary full of students with his hat on (and backwards!) with great responses and great success. Was he "unholy?" **A heart that is willing to do whatever God wants in dedicated and devoted service to God is holy.** Separated and set apart is the definition of holiness we often hear. I want to be holy myself as the Scripture says. Don't you?

Do you think of yourself as "holy?"

_____

_____

_____

_____

_____

_____

Looking at the landscape of culture, what are some attitudes

and activities you notice as patently UN-holy?

_____

_____

_____

_____

_____

_____

Write three practical dispositions or behaviors that you can adjust right now that will push you to holiness so that you might "be holy yourselves."

_____

_____

_____

_____

_____

_____

_____

GO DO TODAY:

Throw something away, delete it from a device, remove a contact or just do something to distance yourself from something that wars against holiness.

REMOVED THE ROOF

Being unable to get to Him because of the crowd, they <u>removed the roof</u> above Him; and when they had dug an opening, they let down the pallet on which the paralytic was lying. (Mark 2:4)

"Pastor Joe, would you pray for me?" A young man asked me this question in Myrtle Beach, SC, in 2006. He was on a retreat with a church called CFA at their Spring Breakaway. I was the evangelist. The answer to his question was and always is "yes." "Do you think God can do anything?" The answer was and always is "yes." I asked this young man who had grown up in a tough neighborhood what he wanted God to do for him. "I want to go to college. I don't do too good at school, but I am a good football player." I asked him what his grade point average was. I was shocked at the number. I thought it impossible to achieve unless you simply didn't show up to school and he was a faithful attendant. He wasn't kidding that academics had greatly challenged him. I prayed for <u>Dwyan Luckey</u> (Disclaimer: I received Dwyan's permission to share this story in this fashion and he verified these facts). After the prayer I said, "Dwyan, I want you to have my personal phone number. I don't know why I am giving this to you. I rarely do this. You call me once a month to check in. I do not know any football coaches in America and just one college track coach. But for some reason I want to keep up with your progress until the answer comes. One month from today call me—will you do that?" He promised he would. And Dwyan did call me. I thanked him for being proactive and assured him I was praying. The next month, I felt a little embarrassed that I had asked this young man to continue to do this; after all, I had no connections. This phone dance happened for several months. Dwyan was very faithful to call. One day after a workout in Huntington, WV, I hit the steam room. There was only one other person in there and I did not know him. I sat and I sweat. Those spaces are awkward places to strike up conversations. For some reason I did strike up a conversation by offering this revelation to the stranger, "It's hot in here." "Sho is," he replied. I continued with a brilliant repartee, "Reminds me of a Georgia summer." The banter went back and forth. "What you talking about, I'm from Mississippi." That was an unusual place for someone in West Virginia to be from, I thought. So after firmly establishing the atmospheric obviousness, I felt sufficiently acquainted enough to delve further. "I pastor a church on the corner of 9th Street and 9th Avenue. What do you do?" He said his job was unusual. I inquired a little more. He said his job was complicated and difficult to understand. Normally I would have left it at that, toweled my face, and hit the shower. For some reason I pushed, "I am a man of average to above average intelligence. Try me. I'm intrigued." He said, "I own a business that searches the nation for good high school football players with bad grades and we get them a college degree." I sat stunned. All I could manage was, "Dude, where have you been? I've been looking for you. You are the answer to my prayer." I felt like dancing. But if the space is awkward for conversation, I am assured that dancing would be quite inelegant. Fast forward many years. From that steam room conversation, Dwyan attended Pearl River Community College in Popularville, MS. He went there to play football chasing a college dream. Although he didn't end up playing football, it did put him on a path. He proved himself there. He attended for a year and a half and then transferred to Western Carolina University. He got his degree and as of this writing, is on the coaching staff at a college in South Carolina. Roofs are protective. They keep the elements out. When destiny is in a house, when God is in a house, and everyone is clamoring for an audience, one can feel pushed out. A roof can become an obstacle. A hopeless man was on the ground. He may or may not have known that a destiny committee was at work for him. They _removed the roof_ so that God could remove his paralysis. At Myrtle Beach, there was a destiny committee at work ready to remove the academic and financial decrepitude of Dwyan. He had never met this man and neither of us had ever heard of a business like this. But shingle by shingle, the obstacles were being pulled away so that this young man could fulfill his dreams.

Write down every obstacle that prevents you from the dream you have.

_____

_____

_____

_____

_____

_____

_____

Think. Has there ever been a time when you saw a miracle happen in a most unusual way—completely out of the norm.

_____

_____

_____

_____

_____

_____

Are you a person that has a hard time receiving help from friends? What would have happened if the paralytic refused the help of his friends?

_____

_____

_____

_____

_____

_____

GO DO TODAY:

When you go to sleep tonight, don't count sheep, count shingles for three nights in a row. Imagine a "destiny committee" standing on the obstacle that prevents you from your miracle. See in your mind a stranger slinging shingles with the name of your obstacle: fear, lack, paralysis, etc.

HIS RIGHT MIND

They came to Jesus and observed the man who had been demon-possessed sitting down, clothed and in <u>his right mind</u>, the very man who had had the "legion;" and they became frightened. (Mark 5:15)

"Don't worry about it Bob. Get your mind right and go back in there and do your thing." Athletes have been encouraged to get their minds right, get their head on straight, and other such things for as long as there have been sports. Do you remember this slogan: "A mind is a terrible thing to waste?" The United Negro College Fund released the slogan in 1972 and it has remained unchanged. The campaign has raised more than 2.2 billion dollars and witnessed more than 350,000 minority graduates. It is a timeless slogan in the American lexicon. These three words found in Mark, "*his right mind*," are more important than a slogan and have a greater shelf life than just a few decades. I know that mental illness is found in the medical charts of many families including mine. Irrespective of disease, it appears that one Satanic strategy is to put people in the wrong mind. Wrong thinking is a colossal waste of time. After a service a few years ago, I noticed a woman talking to the pastor's wife towards the back of the sanctuary. The wife motioned to the other woman, gesturing in my direction. Reluctantly, she approached me. "Do you remember me?" I apologized and said my mind was tired after the morning services. "I called you." That really confused me. "When?" I asked. "Twenty years ago." Twenty years! I had forgotten what I had for lunch the previous day. "I called and asked you to visit my teenage son. The secretary said you refused. The next day my son died. My husband died last year and we have been upset about you." Twenty years! I was stunned and managed this reply, "Ma'am, I know that humans make mistakes. Things get under the radar. I can only tell you that

I've gotten up at four a.m. to drive six hours to visit sick and hurting people. This doesn't sound like me." Her response was, "That is what confused me. After hearing you speak, it didn't sound like your heart." A mind not right—believing wrong information—had wasted decades of emotional energy. I have done some dumb things. However, I believe that dear lady received bad information. Jesus came to put all of us—not just the diseased or demonized—in our right minds. Let this be the year, the month, the week, the DAY of right-mindedness. Let's all of us get our minds right.

Imagine a time when your mind was not "right." When was it and what was happening?

_____

_____

_____

_____

_____

Was anything wasted? Energy, time, money? Articulate

exactly what and how much.

_____

_____

_____

_____

_____

Write a brief prayer asking God to give you a right mind.

_____

_____

_____

_____

GO DO TODAY:

Take thoughts captive. Imagine each one being captured

and processed as valuable or valueless.

HEALED AT ONCE

Then Jesus said to her, "O woman, your faith is great; it shall be done for you as you wish." And her daughter was <u>healed at once</u>. (Matthew 15:28)

[We always feel honored to pray with people that have needs, especially physical needs. The following story has been transcribed from the video testimony of a woman named Heidi. It can be found on joephillipsministries.com. If you would like prayer, email us at prayer@joephillipsministries.com]

We were told by our doctors that we may not be able to have children so we decided to work with fertility medication to try to have a child. After months and months of lots of medications every day, we were able to become pregnant and have our son, Nicholas. But when we decided to have a second child, we started to have the same problems all over again and it came down to taking those same medications every day. After a few months into that I just couldn't take it anymore and I just remember saying to God one day, "You know what, I'm not going to do this anymore. I'm not going to take any more medications. I'm letting this go out of my hands. It's not for me to decide, and God, if you want me to have another child, then I will." We came to church one Sunday and we had a guest speaker, Joe Phillips. I had never heard of him. It didn't mean anything to me and I thought, "Ok, guest speaker." And he spoke and I listened. And I just felt something that day. And he did an altar call and he was calling for people that needed healing. He said a few different things, but he said specifically, "If you need healing for female problems..." and it was just like this light went off. I knew it was for me. He was calling for me. God was going to heal me that day. It's why we had started coming to Praise [her South Carolina church]. We didn't know what had drawn us to Praise. But when I heard him say that, I knew why we were there. When he came to me, he didn't ask what I needed. He didn't ask what type of healing I was hoping for. He just put his hand on my head and he started to pray. And he prayed for a minute and then he stopped. He looked at me and he said, "Put your hands here." He placed my hands over my abdomen. And I started crying because he didn't know. He didn't know what healing I needed, but God knew. We got in the car to drive home and I told my husband. I don't know that he believed me right away because it's just incredible to go to church one Sunday morning expecting nothing and walk away with a healed body. But that day I had heat, warmth and muscle contractions throughout my abdomen, and I just knew. That was the beginning of November and having not been taking fertility medications for, at that point, six to eight weeks, I found out on December 26 we were expecting our daughter. [The video ends with a beautiful girl jumping into her lap. The Lord is mighty to even make people become *healed at once.*

To Him belongs all praise and glory.]

Has God ever done anything for you when you "were expecting nothing" like Heidi talked about? What was it?

_____

_____

_____

_____

_____

If that has happened to you consider WHY it has happened. What are some possibilities?

_____

_____

_____

_____

_____

If you have a big or small need, put some expectation to it.

Say below, "Lord, with expectation I believe you to ...

_____

_____

_____

_____

_____

_____

_____."

GO DO TODAY:

Regardless the background, consider the lengths some people go to have children. Isn't it miraculous for *anyone* to be born? Right now, thank the One who *intimately formed us together in our mother's womb* (Psalm 139:13). Thank Him for your very breath with a prayer, verbalized or written.

HAVING DONE EVERYTHING

Therefore, take up the full armor of God, so that you will be able to resist in the evil day, and <u>having done everything</u>, to stand firm. (Ephesians 6:13)

Our faith walk is sometimes akin to packing a suitcase. If one travels either as a beginner or as a grizzled veteran, thought is required to make our stay functional, if not enjoyable. "Do I have enough clothes? Did I pack too much so that the airline will charge a hefty fee? Do I have my medicine, glasses, a book or two?" That is the way the list may go. Following after Jesus is a bit like that. There are "evil days" that pop up in the lives of good people. When evil days happen, one of the most foolish sentences formulated upon the lips of Bible-believing Christians is this: "We've done everything we can, so it looks like all we can do now is pray about it." Let's analyze those words for a moment. What makes them foolish is the second phrase. Specifically, the timing of the directive. We don't pray at the END of our problem. Well, we do, but we *begin* the problem solving or crisis navigating with prayer. We pray through the thing and we pray, hopefully interspersed with true praise, at the end of the thing. Upon further review, the first part of the phrase is quite Biblical. "We've done everything we can." That sentiment mirrors our verse. <u>*Having done everything*</u> has always meant a sort of spiritual inventory to me. If and when I am faced with a crisis or problem, I usually take an inventory. Perhaps my crisis might be that there is more month than there is money. Financial crises have been common during recession, so I will pick that. The inventory—in no particular order—goes something like this: 1) Have I paid my tithe as outlined in the Bible? A tithe is ten percent of my pay (our family chooses the "gross" pay, because we prefer a "gross" return). I understand tithing may be controversial and that folks repudiate the notion because they do not see it in the New Testament. (One could build a case from the New Testament book of Acts of giving, not ten percent, but giving 100%!) Regardless, this is my inventory and not someone else's. Have I paid my tithes? Check. 2) Have I given above the tithe in an offering? Benevolence or alms? Missions? We have heard it said that the "tithe belongs to God" and the "offering is an expression of our love beyond the tithe." The Bible says that if we water, we will be watered ourselves (Proverbs 11:25). Have I "refreshed someone?" Check. 3) Have I prayed? The Bible has a plethora of promises of the power of genuine prayer. Check. 4) Do I have faith? Mark's gospel tells us we can move mountains if we believe. Has my brain told my mouth that faith exists to overcome the attack of the enemy? Have I expressed my great faith out loud to God and to all the powers of the air that I believe Papa God is big enough to handle the weird moment that I am in? Check. 5) Have I fasted? Again, young Mark tells us that Jesus declared certain evil does not leave except by prayer AND fasting. Have I gone without a meal or meals searching for God's power over my lack? Check. 6) Have I repented of all known and unknown sin? Perhaps I have been a poor steward of God's resources. Repentance means to "turn around" and go and "sin no more." Check. 7) Have I been obedient? Perhaps God has been leading me to call some random person. Several times a day the person comes to my mind. If I obeyed and called to check on them, it could be that in casual conversation, they would have inserted a business concept that would have solved my particular problem. Have I been obedient to everything that I perceive as a directive of God's Spirit? Check. When everything checks off of my spiritual inventory or your inventory, there is only one thing left to do. The only thing left to do is the first three words of the very next verse: *stand firm therefore*. We stand in the power of God knowing that the answer is on the way and coming in the timing of the Father. What we do not do is *sink soft therefore.* No sinking into the quicksand spots of morbid introspection, unrelenting guilt, or futile, carnal troubleshooting. Standing in, through, and over problems begins with *having done everything*.

What is the biggest problem or crisis facing you at the moment?

_____

_____

_____

_____

_____

_____

_____

Write down an inventory including or excluding the above list.

_____

_____

_____

_____

_____

Can you check off the inventory list that you made? Which ones are <u>un</u>checked?

_____

_____

_____

_____

_____

_____

GO DO TODAY:

If you have <u>un</u>checked items on your inventory list, make a plan of how you will check them off in the next TEN DAYS. Write down the plan so that you might declare you have *done everything.*

BEFORE THEY CALL

It will also come to pass that <u>before they call</u>, I will answer; and while they are still speaking, I will hear. (Isaiah 65:24)

M*A*S*H was my favorite television show when I was in high school. It was a show about characters based on the novel *MASH* by H. Richard Hornberger (writing under the pseudonym of Richard Hooker). The show was a very successful program about army doctors dealing with the cruelty of the Korean War while maintaining insane sanity. One of my favorite characters was Corporal Radar O'Reilly portrayed by Gary Burghoff. Radar seemed to have extra-sensory perception. He would appear at the commander's side before being called. He would finish the commander's sentences. He also had exceptionally good hearing. He could hear helicopters before anyone else and he could tell whether or not they were carrying wounded. It was these abilities that earned him the nickname "Radar." It was amazing to see Radar in operation. Colonel Blake and Colonel Potter would turn to scream instructions to Radar, only to find that he was right under their noses. He scared them on occasion. His presence and his knowledge alarmed them. What is *not* fictional is the presence and knowledge of God. The Holy Spirit breathed this promise through the prophet Isaiah. The answer will come before the request does. The hearing and understanding will happen even during the speaking. You turn to yell an instruction and all around you (including under your nose) is a mighty presence. That presence has knowledge. He has information. He has purity. Over decades of the Christian walk, I have heard stories about people being awakened in the middle of the night, thousands of miles from missionaries. They were prompted to pray for urgent and often terrifying "unknown" needs. Later, when stateside, the missionaries would discover that at the exact moment of their danger, someone was praying. So the takeaway from today's three-word devotional is threefold: 1) God is like "Radar." He has the presence and knowledge before we even need an answer. 2) We still have to ask. We cannot lazily chalk up our desperate needs to God's omniscience, omnipresence, or sovereignty. He wanted the laypeople "across the pond" to pray for the missionaries. The WORK of prayer is a real thing. 3) Refer to number 1. The comfort in our prayers is that when we turn to ask, He's already got the answer in His hand. "Radar! You've got to stop doing that!" No, Lord, thank you for your all-knowing, every-sensory perception. Please keep doing it!

Has there ever been a time that God seemed to bring the answer before the amen? No, really think about it for a moment. Have you heard of that happening to someone else?

_____

_____

_____

_____

_____

_____

What does this promise do to your concept of prayer?

Specifically?

_____

_____

_____

_____

_____

Write your current big request. But before you do, consider AS YOU WRITE that the answer may be coming before you put the period on the sentence.

_____

_____

_____

_____

_____

GO DO TODAY:

Just enjoy a greater confidence in the power of answered prayer today.

KEEP ONESELF UNSTAINED

Pure and undefiled religion in the sight of our God and Father is this: to visit orphans and widows in their distress, and to <u>keep oneself unstained</u> by the world. (James 1:27)

We could title this devotion: "Message from the Black Snowball." A blizzard on the road is an evangelist's nightmare but a writer's dream. I hauled the desk in room 324 of the La Quinta Inn from the corner of the room and placed it in front of a large window. I wanted to watch the beautiful snow falling in Northwest Arkansas. Thirty minutes into my work, I heard a snowball hit my third floor window. I was startled and looked up to see who threw it. To my dismay, the snowball was black and it wasn't snow. It was an unholy bird torpedo. There were thirty panes in two side by side windows; three panes across and five panes down.

The right window was bombed by some unseen bird. The top middle pane of the right window had a bird plop about the size of a baseball. Four rows down, the first pane of the same window had one the size of a racquetball. That one was directly in my line of sight. The windows only opened from the outside. "Are you kidding me?" was my general and sustained attitudinal response to this event. I walked outside. There were hundreds of hotel rooms there. I was the only lucky one bombed that day. I had planned on watching the snow and writing for two days. There were no window cleaners coming on Saturday in a blizzard and the hotel staff understandably had bigger priorities during the weather crisis. I asked the management if they had a forty-foot pole. I was willing to do the work myself—happily. They did not. So I had a two-day vista with two recreational ball-sized droppings staring back at me. I decided to write about it. Here are some lessons from the black "snowball:" 1) Sometimes things just happen in life that are inexplicable and cannot logically be brushed away with spiritual platitudes. 2) Sometimes there is literally nothing that can done to correct the things that happen. Like Mephibosheth in 2 Samuel 4 being dropped at age five and becoming disabled due to no fault of his own, things just happen. Now I am not comparing a minor inconvenience to a physical tragedy. I am comparing the suddenness of it. I suppose that day at the hotel, I could have hired a cab, found an open hardware store somewhere, risked the icy roads to get there, bought a ladder, returned with my investment and treacherously scaled the thing to wash the window. I would have lost half a day, lots of money (airplanes won't allow extension ladders as carry on) and possibly my life. 3) A deeper message is a metaphor that almost immediately fell into my thinking. Like that bird's bomb obstructed my view all weekend, evil that is allowed into my spirit corrupts the beauty of God's creation. 4) Impurity cannot be masked over. It is disgusting. 5) Sin will contaminate the view all day.

When pollution is in our spirits we might think that everyone will just notice the beauty of God's handiwork in us, but the eyes will immediately or eventually be drawn to the crud. 6) There are some blemishes that just cannot be eliminated without the help of outside sources and resources. For the Christian, our blemishes, torpedoes, crud, <u>sin</u> is washed by the blood of Jesus (1 John 1:9). For the Christian, the Word of God removes this junk from our souls and spirits with "washing" (Ephesians 5:26). Sin really does distort the vista and it contaminates the way people receive us and our witness. If you have ugly in your life and the window doesn't open from the inside, call on the name of The Lord to bring the clean from the outside. That cleansing extends to every corner within as well.

Without naming names, have you ever run across someone that didn't recognize the blemishes of their lives; you know, someone representing the beauty of God's creation yet not seeing the plops that others recognized easily?

_____

_____

_____

_____

_____

Do you think that you might have ever been that way also? How so?

_____

_____

_____

_____

_____

_____

What is the best way for you to "keep the window clean" so to speak? What normal and regular practices should you adopt and perfect?

_____

_____

_____

_____

_____

_____

GO DO TODAY:

Look in a mirror. Smile wide. Imagine if there was a giant piece of green lettuce between your front two teeth but all day long, no one told you it was there. Now consider it in terms of the spirit man. Go remove the spiritual lettuce that perhaps people see and yet resist telling you about.

A POOR WIDOW

And He saw <u>a poor widow</u> putting in two small copper coins.
(Luke 21:2)

Polly Hardy occupied a room at the Ralston Towers, a retirement high rise in Columbus, GA. She was a retired seamstress and a friend of mine. It seems that someone told me that her career "fame" happened when she made General McArthur's uniform. When she was a small girl she was carried and then dropped by her brother. She walked with a pronounced limp for the rest of her long life. She would sort of drag her bad foot behind her. She is gone now. I believe she lived well into her eighties. I first met Polly in a church lobby more than three decades ago. I met her when I was a teenager and I vividly remember meeting her following a prayer. I went to the altar one Sunday morning and I prayed to The Lord something like this: "Father, I am about to get into a 1974 Dodge Dart Swinger Special with three on the column. I will pull into a gas station and check it for gas and fill her up with oil. In two hours, I have to drive eight hours due south. It will burn half a case of oil on the way. I have five U.S. dollars in my pocket. That will not get me out of the county. Since you are the one that called me to preach and to go to Southeastern Bible College, I thought you should know about that." I got up off of my knees and walked to the lobby. Polly was a true southern belle. She had sort of a Mrs. Doubtfire cadence to her speaking. "Are you Joe Phillips? I've been wanting to meet you, dear. I heard of your dedication to the Lord and that you gave up your basketball scholarship. I've been praying for you." I thanked her profoundly and assured her that I needed the prayers. She gave me my first "Pentecostal handshake." Do you know what that is? I did not, but certainly do now. It's when you shake hands with someone and they put something in your hand. Specifically, money. Why do they call it a "Pentecostal handshake?" Well, depending upon the amount of money received, a person becomes practically *Pentecostal* when they receive it. More money, more dancing and quivering, so goes the theory. Polly Hardy gave me a handshake that day. Since I wasn't familiar with the practice, I at first thought she had put a hard Kleenex in my hand. *Uh, do you need me to throw this away?* She limped off and I looked at the "Kleenex" but it was a one hundred dollar bill. I simply thanked her in amazement. I just looked at the lobby ceiling and quietly said, "From down there (pointing to the sanctuary altar) to right here... wow! You're good. And fast!" During the next couple of years, I had some other Polly experiences. One day I went to box 852 to collect my mail, hoping that there was a letter from my girlfriend, Cecilia. I found an envelope from my home church, Evangel Temple. I opened it and there was a check for $61. I rejoiced at that surprise. Do you have any idea how many cheeseburgers $61 would buy for a hungry athlete in 1983? There was another envelope that looked like the first. I thought, "This is getting more better and more better." That check was in the amount of $1,000. I wept as I held it in my hand. It was an anonymous donation through E.T. Somehow I found out that the checks were coming from Polly Hardy. Polly made quilts with her arthritic hands. She put the money in a coffee can. As she collected a good amount of money, she would put it in the offering and send it to an unproven student named Joe Phillips studying at an unaccredited (at the time) Bible college. Thousands of people have accepted The Lord in the last few years and thousands before that. Polly Hardy gets a lot of the direct marketing "downline" credit for that reality. Jesus saw _a poor widow_. The preceding verse in Luke says "he looked up." I imagine talented writers could write some books about those three words. When he looked up, he saw "rich" people. In the succeeding verses, people drew his attention to beautiful stones and dedicated gifts. However, his real attention is drawn to *a poor widow* and two small coins. I believe he still is drawn to sacrificial gifts, faith, and to people in need. When the dynamics of need, faith, and sacrifice collide, a powerful spiritual explosion occurs! I will never, ever forget my friend, the precious widow Polly Hardy. I regularly thank God for her and though she has passed, her sacrificial gifts to Jesus still live.

Do you know any Polly Hardys? People who live their lives in liberal generosity of spirit? Who are they?

_____

_____

_____

_____

_____

_____

Describe what it is like for people that have been affected by their lives.

_____

_____

_____

_____

_____

_____

If Jesus looks up (and I'm quite sure He does) and sees you today, would your sacrificial and generous life attract His attention?

_____

_____

_____

_____

_____

_____

GO DO TODAY:

If you know *a poor widow*, let the attention of Jesus work through you. Write something, say something, or do something that would encourage them today.

HE WILL GUIDE

For such is God, Our God forever and ever; <u>He will guide</u> us until death. (Psalms 48:14)

The burden came for the first time during my first year of ministry. It only lasted a little more than one day. The next bout with the burden came on my one-year wedding anniversary. My wife and I were fortunate to spend that anniversary in Hawaii. Our first trip (and to date, our only trip) to those beautiful islands. Cecilia's uncle was in charge of all the Post Exchanges (PX's) in that part of the world. So we were around military personnel during the vacation. My heart was really stirred as I mingled among army folk. I felt something of a tug. I wondered in prayer, "Lord, are you calling me to work with the military?" Thankfully, like acute gastritis, the discomfort subsided and it was business as usual upon return–ministering to teenagers. About a year later that "pain," that burden, came back with a rampage and stayed for weeks. I researched what was required for military chaplaincy. I assumed God was calling me to preach to military personnel. I sought guidance from friends, former professors and confidants that I trusted. Many advised against chaplaincy. "You'll be the oldest guy in a room full of twenty-two-year-old officers." "You won't be able to really preach about Jesus." I really cannot remember anyone telling me to go for it with an enthusiastic word of encouragement. So I prayed and fasted but couldn't really sense anything. One Tuesday night, I was making phone calls to people that had visited the large church I served in South Florida. I was so distracted by this burden that I set aside all of my visitor cards and got on my knees and asked God to remove the burden from me or show me the next step. Now what happened next, some people cannot relate to. I am really at a loss to adequately describe it. In fact, something this dramatic has happened very few times in my spiritual life. While in prayer, I said to The Lord, "I am going to be quiet now and just listen." While being quiet and listening, I heard these words—not quite a voice—which seemed more vibrant than any voice—in my spirit very clearly: "Page forty-one, paragraph three." I popped up from my prayer posture and looked around the room and a blue catalogue caught my attention. It was a catalogue from a seminary that had come in the mail weeks before, and I had tossed it in a stack of books on my night table. I cannot even remember ever looking at it. I turned to page forty-one and scanned down to the third paragraph. The third paragraph on page forty-one was a course description, and it said: "PTH 514 Military Chaplaincy." Like a kid on Christmas morning, I ran into the small living room of the apartment and yelled at my wife, "We're moving!" I grabbed her hand and ran into the back and did a play-by-play reenactment. It was done. *For such is God...He will guide us.* He did guide us. I resigned and loaded a U-Haul for seminary with nothing more concrete than the acceptance letter from the seminary. No job. No place to live. His Spirit stopped us in a similarly dramatic way in Georgia on the way to seminary. In fact, we never made it to seminary. We spent five years ministering to families at a church in the same town as Fort Benning, one of the world's largest military installations. We have preached in LaPaz, Bolivia, at an elite military installation. Forty-one naval cadets accepted Christ. We may not understand everything the Guide is doing, but the Guide knows where the tour is going to end. Trust the Guide *until death.*

Have you ever had a burden like the one Joe described that would come in waves? What was it?

_____

_____

_____

_____

_____

What do you think the difference is between a burden and a divine calling?

_____

_____

_____

_____

_____

To date, what is the most supernatural way that God has communicated to you?

_____

_____

_____

_____

_____

_____

GO DO TODAY:

Practice this today and for the next seven days. Set a timer on your watch or phone for two minutes. Say to the Spirit of God something like: "I'd like to hear from you all day long today, but I may get distracted. I know it is not much, but I am giving you the next two minutes. No music, no media, just my shut mouth and an open heart. Do you want to say anything to me?" Then write down anything you perceive from The Lord, no matter how silly it may seem.

COMMIT YOUR WAY

Commit your way to the LORD, trust also in Him, and He will do
it. (Psalms 37:5)

Angelina Jolie directed a film called _Unbroken_. The movie is
about the war hero, Olympic star, and evangelical Christian,
Louis Zamperini, that was taken captive during WWII. Jolie
is not a religious person. It is reported that the last scene of
the film had a big problem. She needed good light to
complete it. However, there was a lengthy storm preventing
this critical scene from being filmed. Jolie, apparently feeling
helpless against the weather, must have decided to follow in
the steps of Zamperini. Louis openly shared his faith before
passing away at the age of 97. She dropped to her knees
and prayed for a miracle. Zamperini's daughter, Cynthia
Garris, told an audience at a New York press conference,

"She was not a person of faith and had never prayed before...[Angelina] said, 'I don't know what I'm going to do so I'll do what Louie would do.' She got on her knees and she prayed for a miracle … everybody saw it." Then the storm stopped. Garris shared something else exciting. "The sun came out, a rainbow came out. She said, 'Let's get this take,' [and] they shot the take. When she said 'cut,' it started to rain again." If that event was a coincidence, it was a mighty big one. It is possible it was totally coincidental, one might suppose. Intentionality is the powerful punch of the Scripture in today's devotion. The definition of *commit* is "to pledge (oneself) to a position on an issue or question." *Way* means "a direction or vicinity" and "passage or progress on a course." I believe God often waits on us to commit stuff to Him. God wants us to "pledge an issue or question about our direction and course" into His powerful hands. So why wouldn't we commit weather, disappointments, money problems, relationships, lack of relationships, academic careers, difficulties at work, ideas, desired success, and the rest of it to Him? Is it because we don't want to sit by and receive the second part of the verse? Maybe we don't want to watch Him do it. Is it that we act like the two-year-olds in the nursery saying, "I do it! I tie my shoes!" I'm old enough now to put aside the childish notion that I can tie my shoes, button my shirt, and stop the rain. I'm getting out of bed these days committing it all to God, and I enjoy watching Him do it. I wake up some days saying, "Can you tie my shoes?" If you find yourself with this attitude, it's never too late to commit. Even late bloomers to the commitment way of living enjoy watching God do the thing He does.

List five things below that you know you should be committing to God.

_____

_____

_____

_____

_____

For just a moment close your eyes. Use your sanctified imagination and think about what it would look like for God to "do it." Jot some thoughts.

_____

_____

_____

_____

_____

Re-write this sentence and fill in the blank: "God I commit my way. Specifically, I commit _____ to you right now. I trust you to DO IT."

_____

_____

_____

_____

_____

_____

_____

_____

GO DO TODAY:

Seven times today, pray that commitment prayer out loud to The Lord.

SO WE FASTED

"<u>So we fasted</u> and sought our God concerning this matter, and
He listened to our entreaty."
(Ezra 8:23)

I peeked around the corner and looked inside a large room with dozens of high school and middle school students. The door with the windows was at the far end of the room, and no one saw me as I observed what was going on. I had just been hired to assume this new ministry. I would begin the next week. A rule of thumb in student ministry is that the "group" should be approximately ten percent of the Sunday morning attendance. This church was running about eighteen hundred in three morning services. Thus, one hundred eighty students should have been in the room I was looking into. I counted sixty-eight. It appeared to me that about eight of them were "dialed in" to what was happening. Eight people expressing any interest at all. The leader I was replacing was more than a capable person. He was more handsome and talented than his replacement. I doubt looks have much to do with effectiveness in the profession of youth ministry. The inequality simply confirmed my self-doubts. The guy was a good golfer, an outstanding technology person, a good singer and musician. These were qualities I did not possess. My inner dialogue that night, as I unofficially checked the room, went something like this: "How on earth am I going to move the dial in this ministry? If that guy has just over one-third of what should be in this room, how am I going to create more business?" So I began the job the following week. I tried to muster, summon, conjure (or any other word) some precious confidence that seemed to be woefully out of stock. Very early into that job, it simply came to me: "I can't do better than the other fellow, and it isn't a competition anyway. The Lord, however, can do more and better than anything I can imagine. Joe, you should fast." Within the first few weeks, I encouraged the students to fast every Wednesday until four p.m. with their parent's permission. More kids than I could have imagined bought into that idea. Once we implemented that simple plan, everything started getting better. The atmosphere of the room became charged with power. The attendance began to steadily go up. A couple of very negative elements in the group—including drug dealers—were exposed and dealt with by the authorities early on. Lives began to change in dramatic fashion including mine. Verses preceding Ezra 8:23 say that the people proclaimed a fast for the following reasons: 1) to humble themselves 2) to seek a "good route" [MEV] 3) for the "little ones" 4) for the reputation of God to the local king. The Ezra account concludes that God was moved by their actions. This devotional entry is not a comprehensive work on the virtues of fasting. Great books cover that topic beautifully. One New Testament account does come to mind. In Mark 9, there is a story about a father with a troubled child. A child with big trouble. Demons made the kid jump into fires to kill him. They forced him to try to drown himself when walking near water. The boy would foam at the mouth and grind his teeth. He would become rigid. It was a horrific flopping display of demonic interference. The father brought his child to the staff of Jesus - His disciples. The Lord asked the crowd what the commotion was all about. Four of the most terrifying words in the entire Bible are in the reply of this dad, "I brought my son to your disciples to cast it out but they could not do so." But. They. Could. Not. Jesus Christ set the boy free. The staff inquired to their leader the reason that they were powerless with an enormously troubled child. Jesus replied, "...this kind cannot come out except by prayer and fasting." You may be coming up against a problem the likes of which make the only sensible response: so we fasted. Going without food to focus complete attention upon God. Not to move God - although God is moved by this. We fast to be strengthened with spiritual power. We fast to position ourselves to hear from God. We fast so that God might give us the "good route." At the end of the four years of working as the student ministry director in that great church, we averaged two hundred twenty-five students. One night, we had a high of over one thousand. Seventy-five students were on the ministry team and all of them signed contracts to remain drug, alcohol, and tobacco free. We took the team to several different countries in the world. That was one of the most successful seasons of life. I attribute it a great deal to *so we fasted*.

How do you feel about fasting?

_____

_____

_____

_____

_____

_____

What are some things important enough in life to fast about?

_____

_____

_____

_____

_____

_____

Imagine how difficult a fast may be. Now imagine the answer to your dilemma after a _so we fasted_ season. Write down what it might feel like to have the problem solved.

_____

_____

_____

_____

_____

_____

GO DO TODAY:

Look at a calendar. In the next thirty days, decide on the day or days to go without food for the sake of a need. Circle the dates. Pray often about it in the days to come, leading up to the fasting day. Then fast for the good route. But today, circle the time—schedule the fast.

HE IS COMING

Before the LORD, for He is coming, For <u>He is coming</u> to judge the earth. He will judge the world in righteousness And the peoples in His faithfulness. (Psalms 96:13)

Dad worked as an insurance salesman when I was growing up. He left on Monday mornings and came home on Friday afternoons. During the week, it was just me and my mom. When I would misbehave, Mom would warn, "Your dad will deal with that when he comes home." We used to have a garden. As memory serves, it was a 700-acre garden. In reality, it was probably a fourth of one acre. Everything seems huge when you're little. My job was to keep the weeds out of the corn, beans, popcorn, potatoes, carrots and such. If I decided to play Cowboys and Indians in the ditch by our willow tree all week, the weeds just piled up.

Mom would remind me of the looming deadline which officially occurred the moment Dad pulled his green El Camino into the driveway. Work inspection. Behavior correction. On a Monday night, Mom's words of warning didn't have that much sting to them. They were not threatening at all actually. Wednesday night, there would still not be much terror associated with the statement. I secretly hoped Mom would develop short-term memory loss. I would steer the conversation another way if possible. Around Friday morning, if my prayer for dementia didn't occur, breakfast time would have a different atmosphere. "Oh no, Father is coming home." Amidst the Indiana corn fields, country roads, and summer gardens, I have several memories of the "he is coming" events. 1) My heart moved from irrelevance to laser focus as the days went by. 2) Dad would deal with and correct my behavior that needed correction. Sometimes it was with a word. Other times with a rod of correction. 3) My work would be inspected. It would be praised if done well. If undone, or poorly done, there was no uncertainty about the action moving forward. The Cowboys would have to wait and the Indians find other activities. I couldn't go fight until the garden was worked. There is a fourth thing I remember. Whether I had done wrong or right, I always loved seeing my dad. I remember a few times he played catch with me. I remember the hugs. The Psalmist promises that God is coming. Regardless of your eschatology, irrespective of views on tribulation, rapture, millennial reign and such, a certainty is that God will come. He will judge. He will be faithful. He will inspect the work and judge the behavior. He will judge the attitudes and intents of hearts. He will hug because God IS love. Whatever is happening in your life right now, let these words motivate and comfort you today: HE IS COMING.

If you are not "getting it done" like Joe didn't get it done in the garden, what day is it? Is it Monday or is it Friday? (Irrelevant or "Uh oh!")

_____

_____

_____

_____

_____

_____

When you hear that "God is coming," does it invoke terror or joy? Why?

_____

_____

_____

_____

_____

_____

What do you hope the Lord says when He comes? If you

don't think he would say those words if he came today,

what needs to change?

_____

_____

_____

_____

_____

_____

_____

GO DO TODAY:

Get your spiritual house in order, preparing for the King's

return today.

NOT BE MASTERED

All things are lawful for me, but not all things are profitable. All things are lawful for me, but I will <u>not be mastered</u> by anything.
(1 Corinthians 6:12)

In 2015, the woefully injured and undermanned Cleveland Cavaliers found their backs against the wall to the deep-benched Golden State Warriors in the NBA Championship Finals. In unprecedented fashion, Cleveland lost two all-star players to these injuries. No team had ever faced tougher odds. When asked about how the team could have any confidence left, LeBron James, arguably the greatest or one of the greatest basketball players in history, gave a bold answer: "I feel confident because I am the best player in the world. It's that simple." This response could be used in illustrating how pride comes before falls. After all, they did lose the next game. However, reflecting on the interview, he was perhaps simply trying to inspire a shred of confidence in his teammates to do their best and not give up. There does seem to be something "Pauline" about what LeBron said. In the above spotlighted verse, the Apostle Paul basically said that he couldn't be beaten. I will *not be mastered* is pretty much saying the same thing. "You can't beat me." What is he talking about? This apostle named Paul was the LeBron James of all things Jewish during his day. He was the foremost authority on the Law, the rules, and the ways of Judaism. Perhaps he was indeed the "greatest Jew in the world." His expression of dominance is different, however, than what the athlete said. Confidence for Paul was not centered in his talent, his skill, and his ability. Rather, confidence came from the work of Christ. Jesus set Paul free from the bondages and legalism of trying to be righteous by human effort. Paul may have felt a bit like a certain German Shepherd from my childhood. That dog had been tied to a tree for a year, and thirty feet of chain was his entire world. When the dog was released in a field to run, it barely knew where to begin with its new found freedom. Paul had been taken off a chain of bondage by the resurrected Christ. He was free to eat differently. He could live differently. The freedom in Christ must have been breathtaking. However, Paul made a determination early on that this freedom came with inherent dangers. Even a German Shepherd in a field cannot run forever. Eventually there will be cliffs, highways, rivers, dangerous ravines, traffic, etc. Paul had this HOLY swagger about him. My freedom will not enslave me. This freedom and these "opportunities" will not beat me. I still belong to God. I still serve Christ, and at the end of the day, nothing will beat me. Surely Paul was reinforcing the truth of another apostle, Peter, who said, "*Although they promise them freedom, they themselves are slaves of corruption, for by that which a man is overcome, to this he is enslaved*" (2 Peter 2:19 MEV).

Paul resolved, yes, RESOLVED, not to be beaten by sensual stuff: eating, drinking, sexual junk. A professional counselor told a friend of mine once, "Yes, you made mistakes, but you have to DETERMINE to simply do the NEXT RIGHT THING." Same concept. Maybe today you need to swagger a bit with a Jesus swagger and say, "Depression won't beat me. Neither will insecurity, fear, habits, appetites, substances, poor self-image, the curses from so-called authorities, or the disloyalty of friends. Nothing will beat me! I am HIS!"

Read these verses. *"For I am convinced that neither death nor life, neither angels nor demons, neither the present nor the future, nor any powers, neither height nor depth, nor anything else in all creation, will be able to separate us from the love of God that is in Christ Jesus our Lord"* (Romans 8:38-39 NIV). List below, in bullet point form, everything God has mastered on your behalf.

_____

_____

_____

_____

_____

_____

_____

_____

_____

_____

What do you need to cooperate with God to "beat down" and master today? Is it freedom from laziness? Is it Satanic distraction? List an enemy, or eight enemies, that you need to rise up against today.

_____

_____

_____

_____

_____

In your heart, do you believe that this swagger—"*not be mastered*"—is a one-time event, a daily event, or both? Why?

_____

_____

_____

_____

_____

GO DO TODAY:

Write in this book or elsewhere a "manifesto." Write down some short and simple sentences of what you will not be beaten by because of the blood and work of Jesus Christ—the crucified and resurrected champion of mankind.

ENCOURAGE ONE ANOTHER

"But <u>encourage one another</u> day after day, as long as it is still called "Today," so that none of you will be hardened by the deceitfulness of sin."
(Hebrews 3:13)

"Therefore <u>encourage one another</u> and build up one another, just as you also are doing."
(1 Thessalonians 5:11)

The article is from the Tuesday, July 19, 1984 Columbus, Georgia Ledger Enquirer newspaper. It is entitled "Nearly Saved, Man Dies After Call to 'Jump!'" I have had this old article in my files for literally more than three decades. It's about a man named Sam that ended his life. Here is the first paragraph. "A distraught man who leaped to his death from a 175-foot bridge might have been saved if a bystander had not shouted 'Jump!' at a moment when he seemed to be wavering, police said." The article goes on to reveal that the identity of the bystander still evaded authorities. The police chief suspected that if no one would have said "jump," Sam may not have leaped from the bridge over the Monongahela River. Before the fateful jump, two police officers arrived. The twenty-five-year-old Sam told them, "I have a lot of problems and the only way out is to jump." The officers nearly had the situation contained. One of them asked Sam for a cigarette. Sam gave him one. The officer asked for a match. Sam extended one leg and put his foot on the sidewalk of the bridge in order to get his hand into his pants pocket. "Come on and have a cigarette with me," the officer requested. Sam was bringing his other leg over the railing to stand on the sidewalk when a person on the tracks below yelled, "Jump!" Sam stood up, looked at the one taunting, glanced back at the officer, and stepped off the railing.

"Sam" walks past us in the grocery store. He sits on the row in front of us at church. He gets off the school bus in our neighborhood. He has "a lot of problems and the only way out is to jump." The officers were doing what the verses above admonish us to do—*encourage one another*. They had nearly encouraged Sam to life, but the discourager was at work. They are always at work. They are the anti-Barnabas. Barnabas is a New Testament character that means "son of encouragement." That is who the world needs more than ever. Satan has positioned many people in Sam's path to scream "jump!" Barnabas may not offer to smoke with Sam, but Barnabas offers to be involved in Sam's situation. "You can do it! Life is worth living. People need you. It will get better. God has a plan." Come beside a Sam as soon as you can. Let them know that they might not have experienced their finest hour, but a fine hour is just around the corner. I have noticed in ministry that men and women who do stupid stuff get scarlet letters, and people yell "unclean" as they approach. Sam still has some gas in the tank. Let's keep him on the road.

Thanks for reading this little book. I leave you with a poem the Spirit led me to write on a Delta Airlines napkin while flying into Orlando to perform comedy. I hope it encourages you today.

TAINTED

By Joe Phillips

Out of the ashes of a devastated soul,

Through the smoke clearing vistas of sinful toll -

Steps the Christian written off long ago.

Publicly disgraced for his prodigal show.

He landed on the heap of Christians tainted;

His shame was broadcast and the faithful fainted.

No one gets a pass from this nebulous shadow.

How's he even standing in this infamous meadow?

Settling in this sediment of black despair,

Barely could the Christian gasp hope's sweet air.

But a voice settled with him, though he could barely hear it.

The whisper of one dwelling with a contrite spirit.

And the voice said, "Stand, Grace has come for you…

Grace has brought life, the way, and the truth."

By faith he took one step on broken reputations.

Each step that followed brought kind confirmation.

Like Samson at his end, a glory has returned.

Redemption is delivered to a man once spurned.

Walking back to a ministry, though not the same -

Chiseled to simplicity by despair and shame.

The Christian, now humbled, walks out from the ashamed.

God's mercy has re-clothed him and he has been

renamed.

Outcast he is no longer for he has been rescued.

A minister once more – a man for God to use.

Jot down a place and time when you experienced encouragement that kept you going.

_____

_____

_____

_____

_____

_____

Do you think (and don't be humble about this) that you have ever been used to encourage a person in a way that made a huge difference in their life? Who, when?

_____

_____

_____

_____

_____

_____

What are some specific ways and words that are tools to encourage a person? List a name, or six names, that might need someone to say "you can make it" in the midst of a crowd screaming "jump!"

_____

_____

_____

_____

_____

_____

_____

GO DO TODAY:

Look at the above list and determine just one person that you can encourage in the next forty-eight hours and in at least one way. Then do it!

Made in the USA
Columbia, SC
08 June 2021